WEB WISDOM

How to Maintain Your Privacy Online

Alison Morretta

Cavendish Square

New York

Published in 2015 by Cavendish Square Publishing, LLC
243 5th Avenue, Suite 136, New York, NY 10016

First Edition

Website: cavendishsq.com

This publication represents the opinions and views of the author based on his or her personal experience, knowledge, and research. The information in this book serves as a general guide only. The author and publisher have used their best efforts in preparing this book and disclaim liability rising directly or indirectly from the use and application of this book.

CPSIA Compliance Information: Batch #WW15CSQ

All websites were available and accurate when this book was sent to press.

Library of Congress Cataloging-in-Publication Data

Morretta, Alison.
How to maintain your privacy online / Alison Morretta.
pages cm. — (Web wisdom)
Includes bibliographical references and index.
ISBN 978-1-50260-187-2 (hardcover) ISBN 978-1-50260-186-5 (ebook)
1. Internet—Safety measures—Juvenile literature. 2. Online etiquette—Juvenile literature. 3. Privacy, Right of—Juvenile literature. I. Title.

TK5105.875.I57M663 2015
004.67'80289—dc23

2014020436

Editor: Andrew Coddington
Senior Copy Editor: Wendy A. Reynolds
Art Director: Jeffrey Talbot
Designer: Douglas Brooks
Senior Production Manager: Jennifer Ryder-Talbot
Production Editor: David McNamara
Photo Research by J8 Media

Printed in the United States of America

Contents

CHAPTER 1

Getting Personal:
Why Online Privacy Matters

The Internet has fundamentally changed the way our society works: We communicate differently, we learn differently, and we go about our daily lives differently. While the digital age has opened up endless possibilities, it has also brought with it many new problems. All the bad things that criminals do in real life can now be done anonymously online, and with technology evolving so quickly, it is getting harder and harder to catch them.

While no one is immune to the dangers of the Internet, kids and teens are at greater risk. Online hackers, scammers, and predators know everything there is to know about the Internet, and prey on young people who either don't know any better or don't understand the consequences of what they are doing. Kids and teens bully each other because they think that what they do on the Internet is anonymous and will not affect them in "offline" life.

In order to fight these dangers, everyone—adults and kids alike—has to commit to being a good digital citizen, which means using the Internet wisely, responsibly, and productively. There are a lot of things you can do to keep yourself safe, but first you need to know why it is so important to maintain your privacy online.

Protecting Yourself

With all the different ways to connect with people online, it is easy to give away too much information about yourself. You wouldn't let a stranger read your diary, look at your photo albums, or tell them any private information about yourself, and yet millions of people allow strangers to do so every day over the Internet. Without the proper precautions, everything you put on the Internet could be public, and once you put it out there, it never goes away.

Your first priority when you use the Internet should always be your personal well-being. There are many people in the world who use the Internet to commit very serious, very dangerous crimes, and young people are often their number-one target. The person you are talking to online could pretend to be anyone, and they use their anonymity and their skills to take advantage of unsuspecting people who are just trying to make a friend. There is a terrifying number of children who have been exploited, attacked, abducted, or worse because they got involved with the wrong person online. It is not an exaggeration to say that protecting yourself on the Internet can be a matter of life and death.

Sadly, even people that you know and trust in real life can use what you put on the Internet to hurt you. **Cyberbullying**, or using the Internet to harass another, has become very common, and the most damaging forms of online bullying come from people whom the victims know. Something that may seem harmless, such as gossiping online with a friend or posting an embarrassing or inappropriate photo of someone else, can spiral out of control and ruin people's lives. In the worst cases, cyberbullying

Text messaging is a common method used by cyberbullies to taunt and harass their victims.

can be directly responsible for a young person committing suicide. It's not just the victims whose lives are destroyed either—the bullies can be expelled from school, lose job opportunities or college acceptances, and even face criminal charges for their actions.

Protecting Your Property

With the amount of information we put online and the amount of time the average person spends on the Internet, our computers and mobile devices have become almost extensions of ourselves. It is important to keep your devices safe, just like it is important to protect your body and your mind. If you don't take security measures to protect your possessions, there are people in the world who are

Computer files infected with malware come in many forms and can damage your computer and steal your personal information.

ready and waiting to steal your information and use it for their own gain.

Identity theft is one of the most serious problems to emerge in the digital age and has caused countless disruptions in millions of people's lives. Identity theft occurs when someone steals a person's personal information (such as full name, birthday, address, Social Security number, credit card information, bank information, personal identification numbers, and passwords) and uses it to impersonate you. Since you can't have credit cards until you are eighteen, these thieves will store your information until they can use it. While you're busy celebrating your eighteenth birthday, they will be busy opening, and using, accounts in your name.

Identity theft can affect your **credit score**, which is the number that credit reporting companies assign to you to determine your credit worthiness. Your credit score reflects how responsible you are with money, and credit card companies and banks use it to decide if they should lend you money and how much. Credit scores are important for people looking to take out loans for a car or a home. Even for victims of identity theft, it is extremely difficult to repair a credit score once it has been damaged. Your computer may also contain credit card information belonging to your parents, and an identity thief could just as easily target their information.

One of the simplest ways for a criminal to steal from you is through software called **malware**, which is designed to damage or access data. While this is most common on computers, with the increased popularity of smartphones and downloadable applications, hackers have started writing code for malware that can take over your phone as well.

Protecting Your Reputation

Depending on how you present yourself, the way you interact with others and the things you post on the Internet can negatively affect your reputation, both in the present and in the future. Things you put out in cyberspace do not just disappear, even after you delete them. You have no way of knowing if someone saved or took a screenshot of something you posted and then forwarded it to others. Even if you delete something from a website, blog, or other online location, it does not disappear right away. It is stored in **cache memory** and can be accessed for a period after deletion. Web browsers use caching to store copies of web pages so that they can be accessed more quickly in a search. Search engines keep these copies until the cache is updated, and during that time people can still view your page as it was before you deleted the content.

It is easy to think that the things you post online and the photos and videos you share are just for your friends, and that you can keep your private life private. This is, sadly, not the case most of the time. Even people you trust can use things you post online against you. If you send an inappropriate picture to a boyfriend or girlfriend, they can make it public if you break up. If you share a photo with a friend that you don't want anyone else to see, he or she could forward it to people if you get in a fight. With all the social media and messaging options out there, there is no limit to the damage people can do if they get hold of something you thought would stay private. All it takes is a few seconds and your parents, teachers, classmates, and even complete strangers can access something they were never meant to see or read.

This breach in privacy is especially dangerous in the case of inappropriate photos, since there are websites where a person can anonymously post pictures and include your full name, address, school, age, and any other information they know about you. Online predators use these sites to find their victims, and cyberbullies use them to embarrass and shame people. Since most of these sites are hosted in other countries, it is almost impossible to have the photos removed once they are posted. Even if you do get it removed, many people may have already saved it and shared it with others.

Posting or texting inappropriate things can cause you embarrassment and encourage bullying (and in the worst cases, put you in physical danger),

WHAT IS MALWARE?

Short for "malicious software," malware is a program designed to access and infect your computer. These programs can erase or corrupt files, steal personal and financial information, and monitor activity (including exactly what websites you go to and what you type), among other things. There are four basic types of malware:

- **Viruses** A virus is a piece of computer code that is attached to an **executable file** (usually a program or a document). A virus installs itself on a computer and can self-replicate (make copies of itself). It attaches these copies to your computer files and spreads when you share files with others.

- **Worms** Similar to a virus, a worm is transmitted by executable files and can install and replicate itself on your computer, but it can spread on its own using a but it also has more long-term effects. When you apply for schools and jobs in the future, the people who review your applications will search for you online to see what else they can find out about you. While you may not think that it is morally right for them to do this, it is a common practice in the digital age, and they are legally allowed to search for anything you make public on the Internet. If they see even one thing that makes them question your character or judgment, you could be rejected.

computer network and does not need to be attached to anything.

- **Trojan horses** A Trojan horse is malware disguised as a harmless or helpful program (commonly in pop-up ads), which tricks the user into installing it by looking and sounding realistic. Trojans cannot copy themselves.

- **Spyware** This type of malware is especially dangerous, since it allows data to be secretly transferred from your computer to someone else's. Often attached to files downloaded from peer-to-peer (P2P) networks, spyware enables someone to steal your personal information (including your passwords and usernames) and financial information, as well as record your keystrokes (what you type) and what websites you visit.

password

CHAPTER 2

Building Boundaries:
How Do You Do It?

While not all of the dangers on the Internet are preventable, there are many things you can do to stay safe online. Before you even connect your computer to the Internet, you should have antivirus software installed, and both your Internet connection and your computer should be password-protected.

Protecting Your Personal Information

The single most important thing you can do to stay safe online is to keep your personal information to yourself. Your full name, home address, phone number, gender, birthday, school, Social Security number, the names of your family members, and passwords should all be kept private. If you are eighteen or over, you must protect your credit card and banking information; if you are younger, the same goes for any financial information your parents have given you permission to use.

The only places online where it is safe to enter this type of sensitive information are secure websites, which use a process called encryption to protect user data. You will know if a website is secure if the URL starts with "https:" and you see a lock icon somewhere on your browser. If you click on the lock, it will show you information verifying that the site is secure. Even if it is, check with a parent before you give out your name, address, phone number, or any credit card information.

Emails, Names, and Passwords

When creating an email address, you should not include any identifying information. While it is

The lock symbol and "https" URL designate that a site is secure and stores all user information safely.

not advisable, many young people do use their full name in their primary email account—if you do this, you should only use this email account to communicate with your family and people that you know in real life. It is better to use this type of email address when you are older, since you will be using email for business and it is considered professional to use your name.

It may seem overwhelming, but you should maintain a separate email account (that is not connected to your primary account) for each social media site, website, or blog that you use. When creating your alternate emails and your screen names, follow the same rules as above and do not include personal details about yourself. You should also make sure that you use a different password for each site

Using a separate email address for each social media site you use can help protect your information.

and email account. Passwords should be longer than eight characters and contain letters (both upper- and lowercase), numbers, and even symbols.

Making Friends Online

Online chat rooms and instant messaging services make connecting with people quick and easy, and it has become more and more common for young people to form friendships online. These relationships can be very rewarding since it is so easy to meet people who share the same interests as you. However, you need to be incredibly careful when talking to people whom you do not know in real life. The first thing to remember is that the person you are talking to could be anyone, and

Facebook makes it easy to connect with people online, but it is important to adjust your privacy settings to protect your personal photos as well as other information about yourself and your friends.

there are many people who use the anonymity of the Internet to create fake identities and take advantage of others.

Be wary of talking to strangers online, and remember that there is never a good reason for an online friend to ask for any identifying information about you. Online friendships should stay online and anonymous, and if someone asks you for information about yourself (especially photos), they are probably not who they say they are. You should also never share this information voluntarily, no matter how comfortable you feel with the person or how long you have been chatting with them. Online predators use a process called **grooming** to make people feel comfortable enough to tell them personal information without their having to ask for it. If you haven't taken the proper safety precautions, a stranger can get enough information about you to locate you in the real world. Some are so good at it that they can find you after a single chat session.

Privacy Settings

When it comes to social media, people tend to overlook the importance of maintaining their privacy. What many people forget is that, without adjusting your security settings, everything you post is public and accessible to anyone in the world.

There are a few easy steps you can take to keep yourself safe while still enjoying the benefits of social media.

Familiarize yourself with the privacy settings of a site before you create a profile. A quick Internet search will provide you with information on how the site works, what people can see, and how you can customize your account to keep yourself safe. You should never have your primary email, phone number, or address listed on your profile, blog, or website. You should also never post about your daily schedule, vacations, or anything that would tell a stranger where you are (or aren't) going to be. This information can lead to property theft when you are away from home, or physical harm if a stranger knows where to look for you.

The default setting for most social media is public, so you will want to change this right away for any social media profiles where you will be sharing personal pictures (such as Facebook and Instagram). Always restrict full access to people you know and have met in real life, and do not accept requests from strangers. A lot of predators and scammers create fake profiles designed to look like they are a young person from your area or school, and it may look as if they are who they say they are. There is no way to know for sure, and the risks of giving someone access to your profile are greater than the benefits.

For blogs and websites that you want everyone to see, make sure you don't have any identifying information included in your profile or on your page before you go public. It is especially important that you create a separate email dedicated to any public blogging platform, forum, or website that you use.

Some sites, such as Facebook and Tumblr, have age restrictions and do not allow anyone under the age of thirteen to use them. This is because of a law called the Children's Online Privacy Protection Act (COPPA), which prevents companies from collecting personal information from children. If you are under thirteen, you must ask permission from a parent or guardian to use age-restricted sites. Even

It is important that your parents and guardians are aware of what you're doing online. You should always get permission to use social media sites and to make online purchases.

with permission, these websites have the right to terminate your account for violation of their terms of service.

Protecting Your Reputation

The things we post on the Internet are forever, and everyone needs to remember that our online reputations are just as important as our real world reputations. Always think before you send a text, write an email or a post, or post a picture or a video. Even if you have your privacy settings secure, some people will see it, and there is always the possibility that it will be saved and spread around. Once something is out there, you can't take it back, and you should always stop and think about who could potentially see what you are posting.

Ask yourself a few questions before you put content on the web. Would this get me in trouble at home or at school? Would I want someone I didn't know—such as a college admissions officer, a law enforcement official, or a potential employer—to see it? Would I be ashamed or embarrassed if it got spread around? Does it reveal any personal information I don't want a stranger to know? If the answer to any of these questions is "yes," don't put it online.

A growing problem among kids and teens is the exchange of inappropriate or suggestive images and videos. If you ever receive a picture or video that makes you feel uncomfortable, or if someone asks you for something like this, speak to your parents, your guardian, or a trusted adult. You should never send or forward one of these messages or pictures. Although you might only send it to one person you trust, you really have no control over who else is going to see it. Also, sending pictures such as these is illegal. Many kids under the age of eighteen have gotten into serious legal trouble for taking inappropriate images of themselves and sending them to others. Doing so is considered the possession and distribution of child pornography, a crime that law enforcement takes very seriously.

Whenever you take photos of yourself to send to others or post online, make sure that the picture is appropriate for everyone to see.

CHAPTER 3

Taking Control: Maintaining Your Privacy

Taking basic security measures is a crucial step toward maintaining your privacy and your reputation, but there are other important things you can do. By using the Internet as safely and responsibly as you can, you are creating a more positive environment for everyone else.

Creating Better Screen Names and Passwords

It may seem like a lot of work to create separate emails, passwords, and usernames for all your accounts, and many people are tempted to use only one or two so that they can remember them. While this is certainly easier to do, it leaves you vulnerable. If someone learns or guesses your password, they now have access to all your accounts. If you have provided too much information in your email or screen name and someone figures out who you are, they can now search all of your online profiles to get even more information about you.

To choose a safe screen name, never use your full name—it is better to use a nickname or a shortened version. You should avoid anything that reveals your gender, age, location, school, or any part of your birthday (especially the year). A fun way to come up with a screen name that fits your personality without revealing your identity is to use a random name generator website. There are many sites, such as SpinXO (**spinxo.com**), that will give you names in specific categories that fit your interests. Make sure you choose names that are not too similar to your own.

Creating strong passwords is one of the smartest things you can do to protect yourself online. Passwords should be over eight characters,

It is important to stay as anonymous as possible on the Internet, and that includes keeping your screen names and passwords free of personal information.

Creating smart screen names and strong passwords is a necessary step toward protecting yourself on the Internet.

and use a combination of uppercase and lowercase letters, numbers, and symbols. Never use any names, places, or numbers that could be easily guessed. It is also smart to break up letters and numbers. One way to create a strong password is to choose a phrase—for example, "I want to stay safe on the web"—and then use the first letter of each word, mixed with random numbers and characters. You can also replace letters with numbers, like "2" for "to" and "0" for "on"—"I want to stay safe on the web" can easily become "iW2sS0tW"—and adding symbols in between letters and numbers will make your password longer and even harder to crack.

Using a single document on your computer to keep track of your emails, usernames, and passwords is easy, but this is not a safe way to protect yourself. If you do use a document, you need to password-protect both your computer and the individual file. It is better to print out a document (or better, use a few different documents) and keep them in a diary, lockbox, or otherwise safe place where only you and your parents can access them. This sounds like a lot of trouble to go through, but taking these steps will keep you safe from all kinds of online dangers.

Avoiding Online Scams

Even if you have taken all the security precautions you can, you can still become a victim of an online scam if you don't know what to look for. A very common type is **phishing**, or tricking people into giving their information away. Phishing scams usually come in the form of fake emails from credit

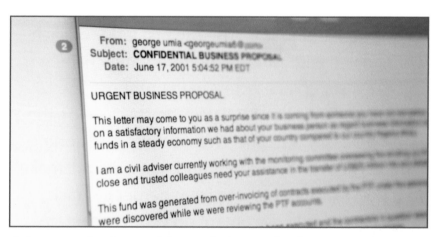

From: george umia <georgeumia@...
Subject: CONFIDENTIAL BUSINESS PROPOSAL
Date: June 17, 2001 5:04:52 PM EDT

URGENT BUSINESS PROPOSAL

This letter may come to you as a surprise since it is coming from someone you have not seen before on a satisfactory information we had about your business person as regards honest business friend funds in a steady economy such as that of your country compared to our country. Together these

I am a civil adviser currently working with the monitoring committee of my close and trusted colleagues need your assistance in the transfer of these funds

This fund was generated from over-invoicing of contracts executed by the PTF contractors and were discovered while we were reviewing the PTF accounts

Cybercriminals often use fake emails disguised as legitimate messages from businesses such as credit card companies and banks to gain access to your personal information.

card companies, banks, and common websites that store user information. These emails will contain a link and ask you to either provide or confirm your information. These emails look very realistic and often use scare tactics to try and get you to give your information, claiming that your account information has been compromised or that your account will be closed if you don't provide personal information.

Internet scams can also come in the form of fake contests or giveaways, and the link will ask you to enter your personal information to claim your prize. Scammers also use pop-up ads claiming to offer you fast, easy money if you enter your information, or get your credit card information by asking you to pay a small amount up front for services. You should never click a link in a pop-up ad, and you can easily avoid this by using your web browser's pop-up blocker feature.

To avoid email scams, first make sure the spam filter in your account is activated. While this can catch many of these types of emails, a scam email may slip through and appear in your inbox. If you receive a strange email from someone you don't know, especially one containing a link, you should not open it. Never click on a link in one of these emails. If the email is from a company or website that you do use, you should go directly to the site without using the link. Real companies will never ask for your information via email, and any urgent problems with your account can be dealt with on their secure website.

Be a Better Presence Online

There are some things about social media that a lot of people don't know or ignore in the terms of service agreements. For example, did you know that many Facebook games and applications can access and use your personal information if you click "Allow"? Even if you have your privacy settings locked down, these third-party apps can now see your information, and sometimes can also access your friends' information.

Another hidden feature that can cause problems lies in the photos you take with your phone. Even if you don't post anything about where you are, when you use your mobile phone to take pictures, the device uses a process called **geotagging** to automatically store data on exactly where and when the photo was taken. It then embeds that data into the photo file so that when you share it, other people can access it. They can even use the latitude and longitude coordinates to see exactly where you are using Google Earth. You can disable this feature on your phone, and you should do so if you plan on sharing personal photos anywhere online.

In addition to your own privacy, you have a responsibility to respect the privacy of others as well. Just because you might want to post a photo doesn't mean that your friends or family members want that photo posted. You should always ask permission before posting a photo or tagging your friends online, and if someone untags the photo or asks you to take it down, you should respect their wishes.

Protecting your friends' privacy online is just as important as protecting your own, so always ask everyone's permission before you post or text a group photo.

Pop-ups claiming you have won a prize or a contest are designed to trick people into clicking on an infected link, or lure them into giving out personal information.

A lot of blogging platforms and websites allow anonymous commenting and messaging, and you should consider disabling this option. Cyberbullies love anonymous commenting features because it lets them harass and threaten people without any fear of being identified. People also tend to say things they would not otherwise say if there is no way to trace them. You want to keep your blog or website a positive, fun place, and there is no reason to open yourself up to the sort of negativity that often comes with enabling anonymous commenting and messaging.

In the same way that your online presence can hurt your reputation, it can also help it. It is a good idea to keep all your online activities "PG" rated, which means no swearing or foul language and nothing inappropriate. If you post intelligently and you write clearly and correctly, it will impress admissions officers and employers who might check out your site. It can also help to use your profiles, blogs, and websites to share things that you are passionate about. If you stay positive and productive online, people will have more respect for you, and it just might give you an edge over someone else when it comes to schools and jobs.

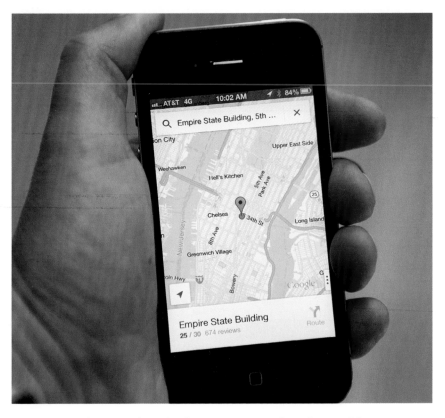

Posting your location by "checking in" on social media enables anyone viewing your page to see exactly where you are.

NETIQUETTE

While maintaining your privacy should be your first priority when you use the Internet, there are a number of important "netiquette" rules you should follow. These also help to keep you safe and ensure that you become a responsible digital citizen. Protecting privacy online is a two-way street: While you may be protecting your own information, you must also respect other's information and privacy.

- **Stay calm.** Avoid using all capital letters when communicating with others online. Typing in all caps is seen as shouting and can offend people.

- **Keep your cool.** You should never send a message or post a comment when you are upset or angry. If you get an unkind comment, do not respond with an equally nasty message.

- **Be nice.** You should never say cruel things about other people online, including spreading gossip or photos that could damage someone's reputation. Being mean to others on the Internet is the same as being mean to their face, and cyberbullying can get you in serious trouble at home, at school, and even with the law.

- **Don't steal.** It is important to respect the work that other people put in to what they share on the web. Taking credit for their work or using it as your own is **plagiarism**, and downloading and sharing files that don't belong to you is illegal. It is OK to share other people's work as long as it is not under copyright and you give them the proper credit.

- **Be clear.** Always use proper spelling and grammar when posting online so that other people can understand you. Your writing skills will improve and you will leave a better impression on your audience.

- **Stay safe.** Never share identifying information online. Make sure any usernames and emails you use for online communication are not linked to anything containing your personal information so they cannot be used to identify you. If someone asks you for this information, end the conversation and block them if possible. If you ever feel unsafe online—even if it's just a strange feeling about someone—tell an adult right away. It's always better to be safe than sorry.

CHAPTER 4

Protect Yourself:
Case Studies

It is easy to think that some of these online threats are extreme and could never happen to you. Think again. There are countless cases of cybercrime against minors. Entire television shows are dedicated to exposing the people who prey on children and young adults using the Internet. Here are just a few of the many stories from kids who were victimized because they did not know how to protect themselves.

Kacie's Story

The tragic story of seventh-grader Kacie Woody demonstrates the worst possible outcome of not protecting yourself online. In 2002, thirteen-year-old Kacie met someone in a Christian chat room for teens and began a relationship with him. He told her his name was Dave, that he was seventeen, and that he was from California. "Dave" spent the next few months gaining Kacie's trust and slowly got information on her, including photos. She gave him her phone number and they talked on the phone in addition to chatting online. Kacie even had two of her friends talk to Dave.

"Dave" turned out to be a 47-year-old man named David Fuller from San Diego, California. Over the course of his online relationship with Kacie, Fuller found out exactly where she lived and had secretly traveled to her home state of Arkansas twice to scope out her house and the surrounding area. The night of December 3, 2002, Kacie was home alone chatting with another online friend when Fuller broke into her house and abducted

After his daughter's death, Rick Woody created the Kacie Woody Foundation in her name to raise awareness and educate others about the dangers of online predators.

her. He drove her to a storage unit in a nearby town, which he had rented during a previous visit. Fuller raped and murdered Kacie before turning his gun on himself to avoid being captured by the police.

Kacie's friends had warned her about her online relationships with boys, but she was a very trusting young woman and always thought the best of people. Fuller was an experienced predator, and was also stalking a few other young girls while he was "with" Kacie—including her friends, whom he had spoken with on the phone and whom he had pictures of through Kacie.

Rebecca's Story

The cyberbullying of Rebecca Sedgwick, a twelve-year-old Florida girl, is sadly one of many similar cases across the nation and the rest of the world. After getting involved in a conflict over a boy, Rebecca was bullied for months by a group of middle school students. They used both Facebook messaging and cell phone texting apps to harass her. She became depressed and started to harm herself, and she had to change schools. She deleted her Facebook page, but when she started using the mobile apps ask.fm and Kik messenger, the bullying started again. By September 2013, Rebecca couldn't take any more harassment. She tragically chose to end her own life.

Rebecca Sedgwick is just one of many teens who have taken their own lives as a result of online bullying.

Mobile apps are popular with cyberbullies since they provide easy, anonymous access to the victim. Ask.fm allows anonymous questions and commenting and can be linked to other social media. Kik messenger is a mobile messaging app that allows texting and photo and video sharing between users. This app is not linked to a phone number like regular texting is, and anyone with a person's username can create an anonymous account and send them a message. Despite the privacy risks, many people share their Kik username on other social media, which makes it even easier for people to **cyberstalk** them. Apps like these provided new and more anonymous ways for Rebecca's bullies to terrorize her.

Social Media and College Rejections

College admissions are extremely competitive, and in the case of a prospective student at Pitzer College in California, his social media posts landed him right in the rejected pile. He friended a current Pitzer student on Facebook, who reported to the admissions board when he saw the applicant had posted negative things about his teacher. Pitzer rejected the student after seeing his comments because they did not want someone who would do that attending their school.

It's not only Facebook that can ruin your chances of getting in to your dream school. A high school student visiting Bowdoin College in Maine used her phone during an admissions visit and tweeted mean comments about the other applicants in her tour group. The school officials who monitor their Twitter mentions saw the nasty remarks and were appalled by the girl's negative attitude and poor judgment. The student was not accepted to Bowdoin largely because of what she posted publically on Twitter.

With all the positive applications that the web offers, there are also very real and serious dangers of which everyone needs to be aware. It is important to remember that what happens online does not stay online, and you should be able to identify potential threats to prevent becoming a victim. Limiting the amount of personal information you post online is the most important step to take toward maintaining your privacy and safety. By following a few simple rules, you can keep yourself and your reputation safe from cybercriminals, online predators, and bullies who may use your information to harm you.

In addition to interviews and written applications, college admissions officers use the Internet to search for information about prospective students. Be sure what you're posting online is appropriate.

GLOSSARY

cache memory A part of a computer's memory where information is kept so that it can be found and accessed quickly.

credit score A number assigned to a person based on their credit history that indicates how likely they are to repay a loan.

cyberbullying The use of cell phones, instant messaging, email, chat rooms, or social media to harass, intimidate, or threaten someone.

cyberstalking The use of the Internet to get information on someone for the purpose of threatening or harassing them.

executable file A computer file that runs a program once it is opened.

geotagging The addition of geographical information, usually in the form of latitude and longitude coordinates, to images, videos, and other types of digital data files.

grooming A process used by online predators to establish a relationship with a child, gain their trust, and get them to give out identifying information.

identity theft The illegal acquisition and use of someone else's personal information to get money or credit.

malware Software that is intended to damage or disable computers and computer systems.

phishing An email scam where a person is tricked into revealing personal or confidential information.

plagiarism Taking someone else's work or ideas and passing them off as one's own.

spyware Software that enables a user to obtain private information about another's computer activities by secretly transmitting data from their hard drive.

Trojan horse Malware that tricks the user into installing it by disguising itself as a harmless or helpful program (such as antivirus software or a system update).

virus Computer code attached to an executable file that installs itself on a computer, makes copies of itself, and spreads by attaching itself to the computer's files.

worm A program that can install and replicate itself on a computer and spread on its own using the computer's network connection.

FIND OUT MORE

The following books and websites will take you on the next step in protecting your privacy online.

Books:

Ivester, Matt. *lol…OMG!: What Every Student Needs to Know About Online Reputation Management, Digital Citizenship, and Cyberbullying*. High School Edition. Reno, NV: Serra Knight Publishing, 2012.

McCarthy, Linda. *Digital Drama: Staying Safe and Social Online*. Kindle edition. One Hundred Page Press, 2013.

Websites:

NetSmartz Workshop

www.netsmartz.org/Teens

NetSmartz Workshop is an interactive, educational program of the National Center for Missing & Exploited Children that provides resources to help educate, engage, and empower children to be safer.

Stay Smart Online—Kids & Teens

www.staysmartonline.gov.au/kids_and_teens

This website provides kids and teens with information on how to safely use social media, as well as how to identify and deal with cyberbullies and other online predators.

TeensHealth—Online Safety

kidshealth.org/teen/homework/tips/internet_safety. html#

This site provides information for teens on how to maintain privacy on the web, avoid cyberbullying, and identify Internet scams.

BIBLIOGRAPHY

Klinkhart, Glen. *A Cybercop's Guide to Internet Child Safety*. Anchorage, AK: SecurusMedia, 2012.

O'Keeffe, Gwen Schurgen. *Cybersafe: Protecting and Empowering Kids in the Digital World of Texting, Gaming, and Social Media*. Elk Grove Village, IL: American Academy of Pediatrics, 2010.

Singer, Natasha. "They Loved Your G.P.A. Then They Saw Your Tweets." *New York Times*, November 9, 2012. Accessed May 15, 2014. www.nytimes.com/2013/11/10/business/they-loved-your-gpa-then-they-saw-your-tweets.html?pagewanted=1&_r=0.

INDEX

Page numbers in **boldface** are illustrations.

ABOUT THE AUTHOR

Alison Morretta holds a Bachelor of Arts in English and Creative Writing from Kenyon College in Gambier, Ohio. She has worked in book publishing since 2005, developing and copyediting both fiction and nonfiction manuscripts. Alison is a writer and blogger and has written a number of nonfiction books for young adults, including another title in the Web Wisdom series, *How to Buy and Share Files Safely Online*. She lives in New York City with her loving husband, Bart, and their rambunctious Corgi, Cassidy.

APR 28 2016

DATE DUE